When Memory Fades

ALSO BY FAYE ALEXANDRA ROSE

Incognito

Mortal Beings

Pneuma

When Memory Fades

Faye Alexandra Rose

QUERENCIA

Querencia Press, LLC
Chicago, Illinois

QUERENCIA PRESS

LIBRARY OF CONGRESS CATALOGING-IN-PUBLICATION DATA

ISBN 978 1 959118 06 0

www.querenciapress.com

First Published in 2022

Querencia Press, LLC
Chicago IL

Printed & Bound in the United States of America

This collection is dedicated to my grandfather, Tom, who I lost before I had the chance to know.

CONTENTS

Foreword

I wrote this collection as part of my master's degree. As someone who often writes poetry, I wanted to challenge myself and write prose. Writing prose seemed oddly more personal—there's nowhere to hide when you must delve into every detail—but this was the very reason I chose the topic of Alzheimer's for my first prose collection. I didn't want anywhere to hide when showcasing its realities and I felt that the short story genre depicted memory loss perfectly, separating each segment in time encapsulated my experience with the disease.

Alzheimer's disease took my grandfather before I had the chance to know him. The one memory I have is him being slumped beside a hospital window only to never see him again. That image has always haunted me and writing this collection proved to be a cathartic experience in unravelling our family's storyline.

This collection is my heart and soul and my family laid bare (with their permission, of course), and I truly hope people with similar experiences can find some sort of relief in the commonality of the disease.

Faye Alexandra Rose
August 2022

The First Time We Saw Him Disappear

"Mark, put the cuppas on will ya?" Valerie shouted over the family, now gathered into a tiny council estate living room for the arrival of the VHS tape of Mark and Gill's wedding day.

"Alright, give me a sec." Mark was flustered trying to sort everyone out.

"Yeah, come on, Mark! The sooner you do them the sooner we can watch the tape," Gill cheered along with Valerie.

"Ah, fine, I'll do it now," He gave up and rushed into the kitchen.

Moments later the kettle could be heard boiling in the distance.

"I can't believe you guys are married; it's so surreal that it's finally happened," Valerie wrapped her arm around Gill before adding, "Welcome to the family, sis."

"Does Dad want sugar in his?" Mark bellowed through the walls.

"Dad, sugar?" Valerie lent over to get a view of Tom who was sat on the chair to the side of her.

"Uh, what?" He appeared disgruntled at being disturbed.

Surprised at his response, she walked over to him and sat at his feet on the floor. "Do you want sugar in your tea?" She lowered her tone and placed her hand on top of his.

"Yes, dear," he sighed whilst rubbing his eyes, "sorry."

Valerie turned to the door to shout his answer to Mark.

"Here ya go, teas for all." He filled the tray with cups of tea that were starting to spill over the side.

"Mark! Watch the carpet!" Valerie gave him a look as if to say, do it again and you're out. She leant over to pick up her tea and cradled it, comforted by its warmth, "Ahhh, that's more like it."

She turned back round to Tom, who was now wiping tea from his trousers with his hands, "Dad, you're a bit quiet today. Are you feeling okay?"

"Yes Val, just a bit tired, that's all," he didn't sound convincing, but Valerie tried to focus on what this day meant for Mark and Gill so turned back to them with a half-smile.

"He's just tired from all the excitement from the weekend," Mark grabbed the remote control off the side of the settee and proceeded to fiddle with its settings until the tape started to play.

"Aw, Gill, look at you!" Valerie swooned over her wedding dress, the puffed sleeves and gorgeous satin train glistened in the sunlight.

"It's so strange seeing yourself on the TV," Gill giggled.

"There's biscuits there, don't forget," Mark pointed at the coffee table whilst looking around the room, making sure everyone was aware that there were biscuits.

"Nice one, Mark, forever a romantic," Valerie rolled her eyes.

"What?" he shrugged his shoulders, "I was just making sure you're all fed. Of course, I think my wife's beautiful, that's why I married her." He nestled Gill under his arm and gently kissed her on the forehead.

Mark began to fast forward the tape through the wedding vows at the church. "Mark, they're the best bit!" Valerie and Gill shouted in unison.

"No, they're not, they're boring. I want to get to the outside bit. That was my favourite." Mark proceeded to ignore their request and held down the button.

Once back in motion, the videographer captured the tall clerestory windows that created a kaleidoscope of colours along the pews. Mark and Gill walked back down the aisle as the recessional song and mumbles echoed around the room.

Confetti then burst into frame, along with cheers from all who attended as they walked outside the grand church doors.

"It's all just so gorgeous," Valerie sniffled.

"Ah, Val, are you crying again?"

"Mind your business, Mark. It's beautiful," she responded whilst wiping her eyes with her sleeve.

The shot panned to outside the church—cherry blossoms danced in the wind; sparkling sun streams flashed as they moved. Streams of pink fell on to the family and friends huddled together for the photographs. Everyone beamed as the camera man proceeded to snap away.

The video panned from the bride's side over to the groom's, both with a sea of smiling faces staring back. The camera continued over to the far left, revealing Tom, standing at Valerie's side, looking confused as to where he was. He looked down at his feet, then back up at the sky before glancing around for familiarity. Mark paused the TV.

"Dad?" Valerie turned to Tom.

"Uh, yes love?"

"Are you sure you're doing okay?" She placed her hand back on top of his.

"Yes, don't fuss. I'm fine, just tired. Everyone's allowed to be tired."

The room seemed to pause as if it were an extension of the VHS tape, until Gill attempted to cut through the silence to revert attention back to their day.

15

"Press play again, then."

The TV still focused on Tom, a vague expression on his face, as a flustered Mark struggled to find the play button.

Valerie lent forward to whisper to Mark, "How did we not notice anything was wrong?"

"I don't know, maybe he was just having an off day?" he mumbled, still trying to figure out where the button was on the remote.

"I'm not deaf!" Tom shouted across the room before standing from his chair and walking out.

Valerie chased after him down the hallway, "Come on Dad, we're only concerned." She went to put her hand on his shoulder.

"I'm fine! Nothing to be concerned about. Now let me go to bed to take a nap," he snapped back.

Valerie was taken aback by his lack of attentiveness. She'd never seen him lose his temper before. Watching wedding videos was a tradition within the family, so the fact that he wasn't engaging concerned her.

She watched him walk up the stairs and whispered to herself, "I love you, Dad," before heading back into the living room where everyone sat in disbelief at what just happened.

"Something's not right, look at him," Valerie points at the TV screen that was still paused on her father looking up at the sky during a photo, "He's usually the light and soul of the party."

"Perhaps he is just tired, Val," Mark tried to reason with her, though not actually convinced of the words he was saying.

"No, I know our dad, something's not right."

"Let's just finish this video and see how he feels when he wakes up, okay?" Mark tapped the empty space on the settee next to him.

Hours had passed before movement could be heard from upstairs. The wooden floors creaked as Tom made his way out of his room and down the stairs. Before anyone could process that he hadn't made his way back into the living room, the front door slammed against the wall, and continued to as the wind pushed and pulled it open.

Everyone bolted from their seats and gathered in the hallway where the door framed a bleak spring day; sombre clouds spat out rain as a cold gust of wind shot through the house. Mark went to hold the door and noticed that the gate was clattering in the wind, it's inside bolt rattling, before rushing towards it in the hopes that he would find Tom still in the street but to no avail.

"Oh, god," he turned to Valerie, "you go that way, and I'll go this way, he can't have gone far."

Valerie scrambled to put on her shoes before running out the door and up the street.

"Gill, stay here in case he comes back, I'm going to go down that way and through the estate," he ran barefoot into the distance through the sodden tarmac.

"Tom!" Valerie shouted through the streets, frantically searching for any sign. Mrs. Norton came out into her garden at the commotion.

"Everything aright dear?" She was still wrapping her dressing gown tie around her waist as she made her way down the path.

"It's Dad, he's gone missing."

"Missing?"

"He's not been himself for a week or so. We didn't know he went out the door until it was too late, I..."

"Calm down, dear. He couldn't have gone far. Do you want me to get my boys out to search with you?"

"No, thank you, no, not just yet. I'm sure he's close."

Valerie pointed up the street as she made an eager getaway.

"Let me know if you need anything," Mrs. Norton raised her voice as Valerie got further away, "I'll keep an eye out!"

The grass squelched under Mark's feet as he ran through the playfield. He paused to regain his thoughts before turning on his heels to circle the field and retrace his steps. He couldn't think through the worry, and the estate that he was brought up in, became a maze. He looked around and saw an alleyway at the other side of the field and ran through it.

Gill sat on the settee clutching a cold cup of tea, swirling it back and forward, before looking up at the window in the hopes that Tom would walk down the path. She toyed with the idea of calling the police, but trusted Mark's judgement so held off. She glanced at the TV screen, now playing static, before reaching for the remote on the coffee table and switching it off. The clock chimed four times. Gill sat in silence, becoming agitated by its ticking, as she waited for the front door to swing open with good news.

Valerie paused for a moment outside Tom's old home and hesitated to knock on the door. It was only late afternoon, but somehow felt wrong to disturb strangers. She glanced to her left and right before taking a deep breath. She walked up the path toward a green door that had a ceramic number '7' plate that her father had painted many years prior. She ran her fingers over the embossed writing before snapping out of it and knocked on the door.

It took a few moments before they opened the door, she could hear pots and pans rustling and the smell of chicken seeping out of their windows.

"Hello," the young woman seemed startled, "Sorry, I'm not expecting anyone today."

"Uh, hi. Um, this, I..." Valerie looked down at her feet and brushed non-existent crumbs off her shirt before resuming, "Sorry. This may sound crazy, but my father used to live here, and he's gone missing—I thought that maybe he could have come here?" Valerie ended with a smile in the hopes that it would sound less farfetched.

"I'm sorry. Your father has gone missing, and you think he's here?" The woman lent against the door, narrowing the gap.

"I know how this sounds, but he's sick and has gone missing. It was just a wild thought that he could have come back to what he knew," she combed her hair behind her ears, "Uh, he lived here for twenty years, it was a big part of his life and I thought maybe he'd have—I don't know."

The woman stared at her for a moment, standing in her front garden, drenched, with odd shoes on, desperately trying to hold back tears.

"I'm sorry love, but he's not here. I'm sorry," she sighed, "I hope you find him; I really do."

Mark had reached a dead-end in a cul-de-sac a few streets away from home and quietly admitted defeat. The adrenalin had worn off and he began to feel the pain in his feet from running across the jagged stones on the streets. As he made his way back home, he passed a father and son bolting out of a house to avoid getting wet. The father placed the boy into a car seat as they both giggled. The council estate Mark had always lived in started to feel less familiar.

The phone began to ring. Gill bolted toward it nearly knocking it off the table.

"Hello? Mark? I'm so glad you called, I—"

"Hi, Gill? No. This is Mr. Bellingham from the Brewery Company. I'm sorry, we had your number on record since that Christmas dinner. Uh, anyway, I'm just calling as Tom has made his way onto our premises. I was alerted by the alarm and found him trying to make his way into the building."

"Oh, God. Okay, is he okay?"

"He seems awfully confused and is in his dressing gown. I think he's naked underneath it, I don't want him walking the streets in this state."

"No, thank you, no, he went missing, we've been trying to find him all afternoon."

"Well, I'm glad he's safe at least. Look, I won't call the police, but if you could come collect him?"

"Yes, of course, I'll be there as soon as I can."

Mark walked through the door leaving a trail of droplets along the tiles.

"Thank god you're here. I know where Tom is."

"Dad?" The news seemed to stop Mark's thoughts for a moment.

"He's at his old job, the brewery, his old boss just called."

"What on earth is he doing all the way over there? Come on, I'll drive."

They walked up to the premises. The warehouse seemed smaller than when Tom used to take Mark to work on the days they couldn't afford childcare. The heavy, arched, oak doors were slightly ajar, Mark pushed open the door and let Gill through. As they entered, they saw Tom in his dressing gown, sopping wet, staring at the floor.

"Dad!" Mark rushed straight to Tom's feet.

At first Tom didn't respond, his lips pursed then fell flat, as if he was trying to find the words but couldn't.

"I...I...I'm sorry," Tom's eyes were filled with fear and confusion, "I thought I had to go to work."

Tom had been retired for five years and hadn't worked at the brewery for over fifteen. Mr. Bellingham looked at Mark with confusion, unsure as to what was unfolding before his eyes. Mr. Bellingham and Tom were close friends for many years but became distant when Tom left for another job.

Mark looked back at Tom, now slumped in his chair, staring at the floor, "Dad, let's get you home, okay? Let's get you warm and dry."

The Vivid Memory

There was a time I wasn't as happy—not long out of the army—my prospects were bleak. The drudgery of a long winter during the last years of rationing. Spam never filled the soul, neither did the soot covered house of my friend who didn't make it. When passing his home, I used to draw a cross into the soot that layered the brickwork. It made me feel like I was closer to him somehow. For a split second I believed that I was, that he would come sprawling out of his front door with his wife, Susan, under his one arm with a couple cans in his other, "I brought out two, one for me and one for you," in his thick northern accent. But the winter's rain eventually washed away the cross, and she moved on to another fella down the street. Life goes that way.

As time passed so did my grief, and the pain gradually subsided. It was now summer or maybe autumn by this point, the details aren't that important. The most important part is the fact that I was now starting to live with a smile on my face. It all started to fall into place when I made the decision to move to a small town in the Midlands to start work in a brewery. I only packed one suitcase full of clothes, my belongings and two pairs of shoes. I left as soon as my notice period was up on both my home and job. I didn't know quite where I was going to end up living when I arrived, but I didn't care.

Working at the Brewery wasn't special, but it was honest work. Most evenings after a long shift John Bellingham and I would pop out for a few at the local pub—it never looked like anything special from the outside, but on a Friday night, the jukebox was alive and so were the people. One evening, I went by myself and walked over to the bar to order a pint of bitter. I stood there in my shabby denim jeans and stained, grey company shirt waiting for the bar lady to pour my pint when I heard giggling to my side. I turned and that's when she caught my eye, standing there all pin curls and sherry. She took one look at me and smiled. I knew I had to do something, so I turned away for a moment to calm myself. I spat in my hand and pushed it through my hair before walking over to her. I remember her smelling of clean washing on a hanging line as I put my arm around her to greet her; it smelled like home, I knew I loved her from that very moment. After ordering a few more pints of bitter and glasses of sherry, the evening started to wind down. Someone put Elvis Presley's 'Always on my Mind' on the jukebox. She took my hand and we swayed for what felt like a blissful eternity. We were left at the end of the night with the few remaining couples—all tipsy and in love—we fit perfectly among them.

***

"Tom?" The doctor placed his hand on his shoulder.

"He does this a lot, we don't know why," Valerie turned to Tom, who was staring vacantly at the wall, "He just stares and stares, and we don't know what to do or say to get him out of it. It's almost like he's in a trance?"

"Yes, well, we will have to run some tests to see what may be causing this. I'm not saying this is the case, but I would like you to take home some Alzheimer's leaflets and get familiar with them while we run some tests."

"Alzheimer's disease?" Valerie was surprised. She knew he wasn't acting himself but presumed it was the passing of his wife, Barbara.

"As I said, I have my suspicions, it may not be this, but I have seen this before many times, and it always starts along these lines. Let me book him in for some tests for tomorrow and we will go from there," he insisted, handing her the leaflets before she left.

***

Her curls were always perfectly in place. I used to wind her up by pulling at the coils and they'd just bounce and fall back perfectly. She often got cross, as if I were mocking her hairstyle, but I wasn't. I loved its playfulness, it suited her. She wore starch-pressed skirts, cut just below the knees, with blouses tucked in, and she was never without red lipstick.

She used to smother my face with smudges, and I'd pretend to get mad, but I never was. How could I get angry at her lips caressing my skin? I once opened the door to the postman and forgot my face was covered in scarlet smears. I'll never forget his expression as he handed me our letters before walking down the path. As I shut the door, she smiled and said my name all long and giggly, "Tommmm," before licking a cloth and wiping it all away.

***

"They think it could be Alzheimer's disease," Valerie handed Mark the leaflets, "I thought it would be more long-winded than this, but all he does is stare, what if we lose him too?"

"I think he's just grieving; we only lost her a few months ago," Mark reassured.

"But he's been like this for almost six, even before she died."

"Valerie, I am sure you're overthinking it; he will snap out of it...he will," he put his hand on her shoulder and squeezed.

"You saw him that day too, you know it's getting worse, whatever this is," she bit her lip to hold in words she didn't want to be true before turning to Tom, "Come on Dad, let's go home, it's been a long day." She hooked her arm with his and helped him as he shuffled out of the house.

"Oh Barb, don't fuss, we'll get it off," Tom suddenly spoke for the first time in days.

Valerie turned to Mark in shock at what had just happened.

"Uhhh…" Valerie stroked his arm, "Dad, Barb, uh, Mum, isn't here. It's your daughter, Val." She smiled in the hopes that he would remember who she was, but he continued to look straight through her.

She turned to Mark, unable to get out any words as her eyes started to well up.

"Dad, don't be silly, you know that's Val," Mark tried to control the situation, "I'll see you both tomorrow, okay?"

25

Valerie turned to Mark as she walked Tom to her car and mouthed, "Come with me tomorrow."

***

Every evening we'd sit with our meals on our laps on the settee. If she was feeling extra kind she would make my favourite meal—steak and kidney pie with mash potatoes with her homemade gravy. We would sit listening to the crackled conversations and music on the radio. We'd make the odd remark here and there about what was being said, but for the most part we would be happy in silence. A friend once told me that was the sign you met someone worthwhile, when you could just sit with each other's company—no bells and whistles.

***

"Here you go Dad, your favourite," Valerie placed the steak and kidney pie in front of him at the table. The steam circled and disappeared as his breath disturbed it.

"Cheers, love," for a split second his cheeky grin appeared.

This eased Valerie's tension. Glimmers of his old self were coming back. Perhaps Mark was right and this was just his way of grieving. She walked over to where the leaflets lay on the kitchen counter and tore them up before chucking them into the bin.

"What's that, dear?" he asked.

"Oh, nothing Dad."

"Valerie?"

"Yes, Dad?"

26

"Where's Barb?"

"What do you mean, Dad?"

"Where's Barb? She should be here for dinner," he pointed at the empty seat beside him, *"Is she at bingo still?"*

"Uh..." She tried to recall what she had read in the doctor's leaflets, regretting throwing them away. Telling them they're wrong about something will distress them, it is kinder to play along.

"Uh. She will be here soon, uh, yeah, she will be here soon, Dad." The wind was taken out of her sails as she lent up against the kitchen sink trying to make sense of it all.

"Oh good, love, this is her favourite."

The Fall

The air felt thick with melancholy. It was one of those winter days where you struggle to catch your breath through the fog. The cherry blossoms once blooming with life stood scarce, the scarecrows stood with crows waiting on their branches.

Mark was the first out of the car, bowing his head to the undertaker who tipped his hat with respect. He was shortly followed by Valerie and Gill. Valerie couldn't look at the church, instead, she looked at her feet and proceeded to disturb the gravel underneath them.

More cars drove up the road and parked outside, family and friends flowed out, making their way to sit in the pews. Mark, Valerie, and Gill followed. As Mark walked up the aisle, he ran his fingers along the wooden pews, remembering the last time they were there. The dim light of winter didn't have the same affect through the stained glass.

"Come here, Val," Gill held onto her hand.

The Lord's my Shephard echoed around the vast space of the church, and everyone stood as the priest walked to his position. Valerie bit her lip in the hopes that it would hold in her emotions, but to no avail. She bought her tissues from her sleeve to her mouth.

"We are gathered here today to celebrate the life of Thomas Pugh," the priest began the service.

Mark stared at the marble stone, it's swirls and patterns mingled into one as he fell into a daydream.

He'd have laughed at us sitting here, crying at his loss. He was a playful character, yet he never liked fuss. "Just cremate me and scatter me in the ocean or something, either way I'll be long gone," he'd often chastise when we brought up death. But really, his final resting place should be with Barbara..."

"And now we will hear some words from his loving daughter, Valerie. Would you like to make your way up?"

Valerie brushed down her freshly ironed, black skirt as she stood up and made her way over to The Lord's Table.

"Uh, hi," she wiped her nose with a tissue one last time, "I can't quite believe we're here. It seemed like minutes ago that Dad was running around, drinking pints and watching football." The room echoed with murmurs and laughter.

"He was everything to me, to us, the patriarch—the glue that held us all together. We feel utterly lost without him here," her eyes started to well up again and she reached for the tissue, "Sor... sorry, um." she looked around the room and her eyes met Mark's. He nodded his head and smiled in encouragement.

"He would hate that we're all sad. He was all for making jokes and messing about," she turned around to his coffin, "I'm going to miss you, Dad, so much. Life isn't going," she was inaudible for a moment. She took a deep breath and coughed to clear her throat, "life isn't going to be the same without you around. I..." she looked up at the ceiling and back to the room, "I'm sorry I can't do anymore. Um, yes, I'm sorry." She scuttled over to her seat where Gill welcomed her with a warm hug.

Everyone stood, as the service came to an end and the curtains were drawn around Tom's coffin. Valerie stepped forward with a sudden urge to run behind them, not quite ready to say goodbye, but she stopped herself—she knew it was time. "Death is the only certainty of life, Valerie," Tom would always say when a hardship arose. She composed herself and made her way out of the church. As she stepped outside her heel got stuck in between two pavement slabs and caused her to pivot and slam her head against the brickwork. The thud alerted everyone to turn around.

Mark ran to her feet and placed his hand over the gaping cut that dripped down her face.

"Here you go," someone handed him a hanky.

"Okay Valerie, we're going to have to get this sorted," Mark placed the hanky on the cut and pressed down, *"I will drive you to the hospital in case it needs stitches."*

"Will she be, okay?" Gill became more worried as Valerie's eyes now rolled back into her head.

"She will be when we get her to the hospital."

"I'll bring the car around," Gill ran into the distance toward the car park.

You've done a number on yourself, haven't you?" The nurse shone the flashlight into her eyes, *"Now, can you please look left? Very good. And right. Lovely."* He jotted his findings into a notepad. *"It looks like she has some concussion, and she also needs a stitch in her head, which I'll sort out for you now,"* he turned to Mark and Gill.

"Thank you, will she be okay?"

"Yes, she should be. We're always weary of concussions as you can never know their aftereffects, but to lessen the risks, I'd like someone to stay with her for a few days as she recovers. She needs to rest."

Valerie groaned as a solution was placed over her cut.

"That's okay, I can do it," Gill volunteered.

"She'll need to be driven home too," the nurse looked at Mark to which he nodded, *"Good, okay, I'll get everything sorted now. Shouldn't take longer than a couple of hours,"* he started to walk out of the room, *"Oh, and if any problems occur, please get in touch with your local GP. Head injuries are complex and aren't to be messed with."*

The Waiting Room

Faye walked out of the toilets, rubbing her hands along her jeans, as dryers never fully dry your hands. She glanced up to see a bustling waiting room, secretaries' phones ringing as soon as they were put down, small talk between strangers and the swoosh of the electric doors sliding open and closed. She walked through the chaos to her seat.

"It's letting in one heck of a breeze that door, ain't it dear?"

"You'd think they'd have a better system than that in a doctor's surgery but what can you do?" Faye responded to the woman. She subtly stretched out her fingers to replicate the woman's next to her. The juxtaposition between old and young made her question her own mortality for a moment. Her gaze fell away from their hands and straight to the brown squared carpet tiles littering the floor.

"I say, the waiting times keep getting longer too. Back in my day you'd just need a strong cough syrup and a warm bath, and it would sort you right out." She sniggered as she gave her shoulder a gentle nudge with hers. The familiarity made Faye smile.

"More people around 'ere, the more people to see I guess."

"Yeah. It's all changed now," the woman stared into the corner of the room for a moment before snapping back, "My daughter used to be so sickly you know, in and out of the doctor's all the damn time. It was such a worry."

"I bet. Children have a way of doing that to you."

"Ain't that the truth dear. I'd have to walk them for miles to come here before I moved houses. It would play havoc on my hips," she scrunched her nose.

"It's all worth it in the end though."

"Yes dear," she sighed, "it is indeed."

"Mr Jones?" the doctor bellowed, and everyone turned to watch a man struggling to get out of his seat quick enough. He leant against the arm rest just enough to grasp his walking stick and forced his bodyweight upwards before shuffling down the corridor.

"Oh heck," the woman whispered, "I hope I don't get that old."

Faye's stomach flipped, that moment where a single sentence silences your entire body. Around her, mothers with coughing daughters on their laps, elderly couples offering each other mints.

"You ok, dear?"

"Yes, sorry. Just lost my trail of thought."

"I do that all the time, not to worry," she smiled, "so, are you new to the area? Haven't seen you around here often, and I come here a lot."

"Uhh...Yes, I've lived here my whole life."

"Beautiful place isn't it. I've watched it transform over the years. It used to be an old mining town; did you know?"

"Yeah, my Mum told me. Growing up she used to take me and my brothers to see all the old digging sights and tell us all the stories," she shuffled in her seat and sighed.

"Oh, that's good. Always nice to know the place you live I say."

Faye suddenly became distracted by a father and son walking into the surgery.

"Ain't that a lovely sight, hand in hand."

"It is," Faye didn't know how else to respond.

The nurse scurried into the waiting room, "Mrs Egglesworth?" to which a middleaged woman stood and followed her down the corridor.

"Oh... where is it? Ah, there it is," the woman bought the tissue to her nose and proceeded to make a noise, a rare moment the whole waiting room fell silent.

"Don't you hate it when that happens," she chuckled.

Faye smiled. Mr Jones made his way out of the electric doors.

"Oh, that's one more down," she nodded her head towards his direction.

Moments later the doctor peered his head around his door, "Ms Proctor?"

"Have you got all your things?" Faye gently placed her hand behind her back to aid her up off the seat.

"Yes, thank you dear," she paused for a moment and looked around, "uh."

"Don't worry, you're at the doctors."

"Oh yes, the doctors, that's right."

The doctor peered his head around the door, "Valerie?" to which Faye gestured that she had heard, and they were making their way over.

"Come on then," she takes her arm, "let's get you better."

Pasta for Dinner

Valerie stood with one hand on her hip, the other stirring the sauce for dinner. Swirling the wooden spoon seemed mesmerising as her eyes were fixed on the pan.

"Hey, Mum," I chime in and break her from her daydream.

"Hi, Darling," she smiles.

"What's for dinner?"

"Your favourite!" Her face radiates with a childish glow.

I watch as she places the sauce on top of the perfectly lined bowl of pasta. We sit down and talk about her day; she speaks of her latest knitting project— a cardigan for the looming winter months. She mimics the movements as she speaks, weaving the thread, fixing the loop and repeat. I watch her in her element before asking her about her plans for the evening.

"I'll be watching Strictly Come Dancing, it's a Saturday night, after all, Dear," we both smile, comforted by the mundaneness of it all.

The cuckoo clock chimes six times; each time the dust sprinkles like confetti on top of the ornaments below. The clock was a moving gift from her mother when she first moved into her home, such an unexpected heirloom that was bought from a Sunday market back in the 1960's.

"Isn't this lovely," she says, "my best yet," she gestures towards her plate.

"It is! The sauce has just enough kick to it."

"Mmhmm," she responds, before slurping the remnants off her fork.

I finish mine first, like always, leaving smears of sauce and flecks of pasta on the plate. I spend the remaining time watching her pick up her fork, one penne at a time, before swirling it in her mouth until it is soft enough to be digested.

37

"Uh," she groans, "I don't think I can eat another bite." She places both hands on her stomach to confirm what she has just said.

"No problem at all, Mum, let me clear this all up for you," I take the plates to the bin, scraping the speckles off one and a mound of pasta off the other. The fork scratches against the porcelain as the contents fall into the darkness.

"Do you think Tom will visit for dinner tonight?" She chirps through the silence with such sprite.

"Uh," this catches me off guard, "he's probably eaten, you know how he is, always out doing something he forgets to keep track of the time." I watch her digest my response, scratching her head, then nodding. I turn back to stare into the void of the bin.

"Come on then, let's get you to the living room," I hold my hand out for support.

"I wish you would stop fussing, Dear," she grunts, struggling to hold her weight on her feet.

She shuffles her slippers into the lounge and flops onto a green velvet armchair, we named the shape shifter—it used to look so big when my brother and I were younger, then it felt too small as our growing bodies sat confined to its frame. Now, it seems to have reverted, swallowing our mother whole.

She switches on the television, tapping the back of it to get it to respond.

"Bloody batteries," she grumbles whilst wobbling it in the air.

I observe her in her 'nook' just beside the fireplace. Next to her is a bookcase filled with stories and photographs—one is a black and white picture of her parents, Barbara and Tom, smiling on a boat in the Mediterranean.

"Do you need anything else?"

"No, love, you sit down. Countdown is on soon," her eyes firmly on the television.

The warmth from the fire fills the room. Its crackles are faint yet soothing, causing my eyes to feel heavy.

I awake to find an empty armchair with the television still playing full blast into the living room. Clambers from the kitchen break through the familiar as I rush towards the noise.

Here is my mother, beside the cooker, having just dropped the wooden spoon onto the tiles.

"These things are so fiddly. Would you mind picking it up for me, Dear?"

"Of course. You gave me a fright; I woke up without you there," I bend down to pick up the spoon.

"I'm just cooking dinner. Someone has to do it," she tuts as she stirs the sauce.

I look outside to complete darkness; with only my reflection staring back at me.

"Of course, mum, silly me. I'm starving."

"What are you making?"

"Your favourite!" there was that childish grin again.

The old cuckoo clock chimes twelve times; each time dust sprinkles like confetti on to the ornaments below. The clock was her mother's, and soon it will be mine.

What is hope, anyway?

Hope can be toxic. It can feel like you're clinging to an edge of a rope as it frays away under pressure. You know it's going to snap; you know reality is coming, but you continue to hold on despite that fact. That's how I felt when I received the news that my estranged father has Alzheimer's disease in the midst of editing this collection.

Living a life without a parent is hard, you're left with unanswered questions that sting, and often a tiny section of your mind is dedicated to them—a compartment of hope—filled with a dream that one day they will apologise for their disappearance, for all the years lost and that you're both suddenly presented with an opportunity to build a bond, leaving the past in the past. I have no shame in admitting I had that compartment locked tightly inside my brain for him and I have ever since my younger self acknowledged that he left.

But how did I find out, you ask? Because of marriage paperwork. I'm getting married in November and needed information on my father to process all the legal stuff. The general information that I should have known yet didn't. But that's not the point, is it? The point is that I found out my father has Alzheimer's disease and has for years, over a Facebook message on a random Tuesday.

The rope that I have held on to for the past 31 years has snapped. The pressure was too much. The glimmer of hope that my father would apologise and that we'd move forward together, gone in an instant. He won't remember me, nor will he ever. You could call it irony; like his memory is trying to forgive him for his sins. If he can't remember it, he never abandoned my three brothers and I, right? However, I call it painful—but what's hope, anyway?

www.ingramcontent.com/pod-product-compliance
Lightning Source LLC
Chambersburg PA
CBHW051002140626
46546CB00017B/2726